YOUR KNOWLEDGE HAS VALUE

NATO, climate change and security. The Arctic missing in Madrid Strategic Concept 2022

Céline Rodrigues

Bibliographic information published by the German National Library:

The German National Library lists this publication in the National Bibliography; detailed bibliographic data are available on the Internet at http://dnb.dnb.de.

ISBN: 9783346877376
This book is also available as an ebook.

© GRIN Publishing GmbH
Trappentreustraße 1
80339 München

Print and binding: Books on Demand GmbH, Norderstedt, Germany
Printed on acid-free paper from responsible sources.

The present work has been carefully prepared. Nevertheless, authors and publishers do not incur liability for the correctness of information, notes, links and advice as well as any printing errors.

GRIN web shop: https://www.grin.com/document/1330079

NATO, climate change and security:
the Arctic missing in Madrid Strategic Concept 2022

Céline Rodrigues

ABSTRACT

In the 21st century climate and security are two intertwined concepts, as it is not possible to present them separately when there is awareness regarding the transnationalism of the impacts and effects of climate change as well as the implications it has in traditional and non-traditional securities. Those two situations are even more relevant in the Arctic region that has been affected since last century by Anthropocene activities and has its ups and downs from world´s attention.

Matching climate, security and Arctic, it is considered that the Green Politics Theory frames this paper aside the securitization of the Copenhagen School allowing to confirm the presence of the Arctic region recurring to the qualitative methodology by analysing NATO´s official documents. The Alliance is always in a process of adaptation to a quick changing world. This time it needs to assimilate that climate change is a threat with security matters at different levels, armed forces included, and that the Arctic region shall be in the lens of attention due to rising competition and conflict triggered also by Russia and China.

NATO, climate change and security[1]:
the Arctic missing in Madrid Strategic Concept 2022

Climate change and security are two topics that are advancing in importance and relevance in International Relations studies in the 21st century. Anthropocene activities are confirmed by the Intergovernmental Panel on Climate Change (IPCC) 2014 AR5[2] as the main factor for what we are witnessing in the first quarter of this century. Ecosystems, of which humans are part of, are being destroyed around the world downgrading human living conditions, rising ocean waters and leading to scarcity of resources. In what concerns the Arctic region, it is the first place to suffer from those changes, being considered the bell for the rest of the world. The Arctic is warming four times faster[3] than the rest of the world and this proven scientific fact challenges security and how it is perceived and understood nowadays. With climate change comes scarcity of resources and competition in a region that has been an example of cooperation and peace as expressed and whished by Gorbachev in 1987 in Murmansk[4]. The Arctic region is back, and tensions and conflicts too. The security of people, indigenous and non-indigenous, is central. This brings something new to security, labelled as non-traditional security.

In the topic of climate change, the Alliance expects "to take the lead in understanding and adapting to the impact of climate change on security" as mentioned in the report *NATO and Climate Change: A Climatized Perspective on Security* (Rico, 2022, p.1). Shall it be remembered that climate change is considered a threat by the United Nations since 2009 (A/64/350, 2009, p. 6)[5]. Over the 70 years of existence, the Washington Treaty 1949, has been challenged to adapt to new contexts and threats. Though, it seems that the NATO, that came back to life and got out of the "brain-death" (using Emmanuel Macron´s expression in 2019[6]) state with the War in Ukraine that started in 24 February 2022, is still pretty much in sight of traditional security.

---

[1] This paper can be considered as literature review of Rodrigues, C. (2022). NATO, the Arctic and climate security: Strategic Concept for a global threat. *Munich, GRIN Verlag.* https://www.grin.com/document/1246666
[2] IPCC. (2014). AR5. *Climate Change 2014 Synthesis Report Summary for Policymakers.* https://www.ipcc.ch/site/assets/uploads/2018/05/SYR_AR5_FINAL_full_wcover.pdf
[3] World Economic Forum. (2022). *The Arctic is warming nearly four times faster than the rest of the world. How concerned should we be?* https://www.weforum.org/agenda/2022/08/arctic-warming-four-times-faster-than-world/
[4] Gorbachev, M. (1987, October 1). Mikhail Gorbachev's Speech in Murmansk at the Ceremonial Meeting on the Occasion of the Presentation of the Order of Lenin and the Gold Star to the City of Murmansk. https://www.barentsinfo.fi/docs/Gorbachev_speech.pdf
[5] United Nations. (2009). *Climate change and its possible implications: Report of the Secretary-General.* A/64/350. https://digitallibrary.un.org/record/667264

[6] France 24. (2019, November 28). France's Macron defends 'brain death' criticism after talks with NATO chief. *France 24.* https://www.france24.com/en/20191128-live-france-s-macron-meets-nato-chief-to-address-brain-death-criticism

After the Second World War, the Washington Treaty 1949 is signed by twelve countries (Belgium, Canada, Denmark, France, Iceland, Italy, Luxembourg, the Netherlands, Norway, Portugal, the United Kingdom, and the United States) known as North Atlantic Treaty Organization (NATO) with the goal of defending its members against the Soviet Union[7]. A security community, in the lens of Karl Deutsch, created by allies that seemed to have the same values and committed to keep and maintain democracy and the rule of law; what would allow to work in a collective way for defence and security through dialogue and cooperation with a specific objective: to live in peace. The world has been changing since its inception, compelling the organisation to adapt and review constantly its strategies and actions. This fact is considered as the legacy, success and longevity of the Alliance (NATO 2030, 2020, p. 7). As such, the organisation is still the unique and essential transatlantic forum for consultations on issues such as territorial integrity, political independence and security of its members. A relevant note here is that climate change does not care about territory and borders. Only by looking at it as a security issue can actions be taken and the regions more affected, as the Arctic, will be a priority.

In order to better analyse the presence of the Arctic region in the Madrid Strategic Concept 2022 and NATO´s adaptation to climate change, it makes sense to frame this paper within the Green Political Theory which has been evolving since the 1960s. This theory can also be aligned with the Copenhagen school (1985). In that sense, the author John Barry indicates in his chapter, entitled "Green political theory", (2014) three moments, or waves, in the evolution of the term green political theory: i) the first wave begins in the 1990´s by identifying "ecologism" as an ideology and green political theory as a "distinctive approach"; ii) the second one is the period of the development of other schools of thought (such as feminism, liberalism, critical theory) expanded debates between those schools and green political theory. It is during this wave that Green theory is recognized within International Relations with the transnationalism question of problems caused by climate change, as mentioned by Robyn Eckersley (Ari and Gokpinar, 2019, p. 166); iii) the "third generation" of green theory is the more recent generation, which interdisciplinary is integrated with practical and empirical research of a "range of disciplines and knowledge outside politics, political science and political theory" (Barry, 2014, p. 4; idem). Scholars have been clarifying the difference between

---

[7] It is relevant to enhance that "This is only partially true. In fact, the Alliance's creation was part of a broader effort to serve three purposes: deterring Soviet expansionism, forbidding the revival of nationalist militarism in Europe through a strong North American presence on the continent, and encouraging European political integration." (NATO. (n.d.). A Short History of NATO. https://www.nato.int/cps/en/natohq/declassified_139339.htm)

green politics - who consider that the structure can be challenged - and environmentalists – "who accept the framework and pursue the solution within the structures" (Paterson cited by Ari and Gokpinar, 2019, p. 167). Consequently, the concept of security, which is also recent in International Relations, changes its focus, placing the people at the center, as objects (human security – non-traditional security, Padrtova 2020; Shiblee and Rashid, 2021) leading states to provide them protection (Hossain, 2013). Consequently, the traditionalist vision is broken when topics such as economic, military, political, environmental and social are identified as sectors of security according to different sources of threats (Padrtova 2020, p. 31; Hossain, 2017, p. 6; Waisová, 2003, p. 60). Buzan, Wœver and De Wilde ´s vision is the basis for UN´s definition of human security[8], [9]. Once the object climate change is perceived as a threat, then it becomes a "security issue only by being labelled as one" (Diskaya cited by Hossain, 2017, p. 6). The **figure 1** below presents the difference between "traditionalists", "deepeners" and "wideners" where the objects are connected to a category.

Figure 1: Five Sectors (sources of threats) and different understandings of security

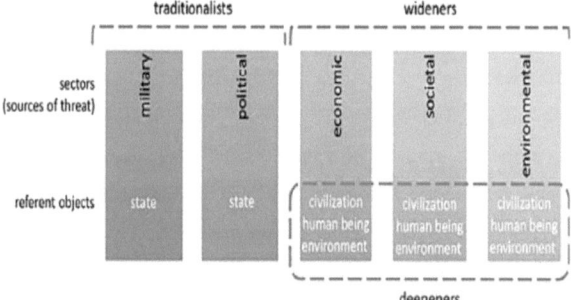

Source: Padrtova, 2020, p. 30

This confirms the link, nexus between climate change and security[10] as mentioned by the IPCC, WGII (2022).

The development of the analysis is to be done according to the qualitative methodology which allows an inductive reasoning through observation and analysis of official

---

[8] See: United Nations. United Nations Development Programme. (1994). *Human Development Report 1994*. https://hdr.undp.org/sites/default/files/reports/255/hdr_1994_en_complete_nostats.pdf
[9] See: United Nations. Commission on Human Security. (2003). *Human security now: protecting and empowering people. Commission on Human Security*. https://digitallibrary.un.org/record/503749
[10] The author of the Belfer report presents a different theory called climatization, climatized perspective on security. See: Rico, L.G. (2022). NATO and Climate Change: A Climatized Perspective on Security. *Belfer Center for Science and International Affairs*. Harvard Kennedy School. https://www.belfercenter.org/publication/nato-and-climate-change-climatized-perspective-security (p. 15)

documents such as *NATO Climate Change and Security Action Plan* (2021), *Madrid Strategic Concept 2022*, Report *NATO and Climate Change: A Climatized Perspective on Security* (2022) and The Secretary General´s Report *Climate Change & Security Impact Assessment* (2022). The analysis is complemented with reports of rapporteur such as Jean-Charles Larsonneur (2021).

The development of this issue will be done by dividing the work in two parts: the first part will give a brief overview of Strategic Concepts (SC) that will give the opportunity to compare Lisbon Strategic Concept 2010 and Madrid Strategic Concept 2022 which appear to be opposing. It will be possible to check how the new document addresses climate change and if recommendations were taken into considerations during the elaboration of the new document and if they were able to match with Climate Change and Security Action Plan (2021) so it is not an isolated document. The second part will develop the ups and downs, attention and forgetfulness in the 20th and 21st centuries of the Arctic and how it is perceived within the Alliance. In the conclusion, it will be possible to confirm that: i)- the Arctic is part of NATO, even if it is not expressed, written in the Strategic Concept 2022; ii)- the Alliance still needs to adapt to a new context in a mix of traditional and non-traditional securities linked to the climate change threat.

1- Strategic Concepts[11]: evolution

The Strategic Concept (SC) is considered a key document, having a second place after the Washington Treaty 1949. It aims to define the Alliance strategy in a military and political way according to the challenges and threats identified at the moment it is elaborated. The aim of developing this kind of document is to be prepared for the future[12]. This kind of document also reinforces the commitment to "the principles of individual liberty, democracy, human rights and the rule of law as well as to the purposes and principles of the Charter of the United Nations, with the main priority of assuring and maintaining international peace and security" (Strategic Concept, 2010, p. 6). Meaning that three core tasks must be fulfilled by all members: collective defence, crisis management and cooperative security.

---

[11] See: NATO. (2022). Evolution of NATO Strategy 1949-1999:
https://www.nato.int/nato_static_fl2014/assets/pdf/pdf_2009_07/20090728_strategic_concept.pdf
[12] See: NATO (n.d). *What is NATO's Strategic Concept?* https://www.nato.int/strategic-concept/

The Strategic Concept is reviewed every decade since the end of Cold War[13]. Since its birth, the Strategic Concepts have been prepared in two historic different moments (the Cold War and the post-Cold War). 2022 might be categorised as the beginning of a third moment. From 1949 to 1991, the strategy was mainly categorised by defence and deterrence, without excluding dialogue and détente in the last two decades of the first moment. During this period four Strategic Concepts were released with other complementary such as "Strategic Guidance", "The Most Effective Pattern of NATO Military Strength for the Next Few Years" and "Measures to Implement the Strategic Concept".

In the second period, the Alliance focused on cooperation and security. The 9/11 terrorist attacks in 2001 moved attentions to terrorism. During this post-cold war moment, three Strategic concepts were presented in 1991, 1999 and 2010 with complementary texts such as MC Directive for Military Implementation of the Alliance's Strategic Concept, MC Guidance for the Military Implementation of the Alliance Strategy and MC Guidance MC 400/3. The Lisbon Strategic Concept turned to be out of context four years after its presentation due to the annexation of Crimea by Russia. Consequently, the idea of peace quickly did not apply to the geopolitical context as 2022 demonstrates. The wish of cooperation with Russia and the absence of China in 2010 is the complete opposite in time being, and are, in June 2022, are considered main threats in the new document. Nonetheless, the concept of security has been evolving and has a holistic perspective. It looks like some results and recommendation, namely report of Jean-Charles Larsonneur[14] were taken into consideration as it is possible to find references to climate change by acknowledging that armed forces are also affected (number 19, 2022, p. 6) and human security (number 19, 2022, p. 9) in the Madrid 2022 Strategic concept. But in a very smooth way of expression.

If China and Russia are named and considered as threats, unfortunately, in what concerns the Arctic region and its safety and security Buchanan´s observation of "lack of reference to that region in the documents, with only one mention to High North in 2021 Brussels Summit Communiqué" (cited by Bye, 2021) is sustained in the new document released in the 8th Strategic Concept presented in Madrid 2022. Disappointingly, not even the Baltic Sea, included in the recommendation d) of NATO 2030 (2020), is mentioned in

---

[13] For more information see: NATO. (2022, July 18). Strategic Concepts. https://www.nato.int/cps/en/natohq/topics_56626.htm
[14] Larsonneur, J-C. (2021, October 9). Security Challenges on the High North. Report. *NATO Parliamentary Assembly.* https://www.nato-pa.int/download-file?filename=/sites/default/files/2021-10/016%20DSCTC%2021%20E%20rev.%202%20fin%20-%20SECURITY%20HIGH%20NORTH.pdf)

the SC 2022[15], when it is stated that "Maritime security is key to our peace and prosperity" (number 23, Madrid SC, 2022, p. 7). I add that the Arctic Ocean too is not mentioned. Though, the document NATO 2030 (2020) in the Proposal number 7 states that climate change is a defining challenge of our days and has security implications in different regions included the Arctic.

Climate change and environment security, despite its recognition as potential threat had occurred in 1969 as mentioned by Causevic, was not officially added and integrated in the organization agenda until 2010 (2017, pp. 72-73) because it is still perceived at a national level. Amar Causevic, author of the article "Facing an Unpredictable Threat: Is NATO Ideally Placed to Manage Climate Change as a Non-Traditional Threat Multiplier?" also informs that since 2010, much have been done regarding environment security and the different Secretary Generals have discussed this subject in different moments:

- 2010 with the creation of the Emerging Security Challenges Division (ESCD) to focus on the emerging security challenges;
- 2013 the Green Defense for more effectiveness and change in use of energy;
- and in 2014 with the Wales declaration and adoption of Resolution 427 on Climate Change and International Security, at NATO Parliamentary Assembly, to reduce pollution. This recent introduction of environment security in NATO's discussion shows the awareness of linkage between climate change and Arctic within the organisation as a matter of security and of protection of sovereignty, not only at a regional level but also at a global level.

---

[15] See: Madrid 2022 Strategic Concept, number 45, p. 11 (NATO. (2022). NATO 2022 Madrid Strategic Concept. https://www.nato.int/strategic-concept/)

Unfortunately, the recommendations below were not considered:

l. to bolster NATO's situational awareness in the Arctic region, including through greater information sharing, the creation of a working group on the Arctic, and training and exercises, and to maintain a good dialogue with Allies about search and rescue capabilities in the region;

m. to fully recognise climate change-related risks as significant threat multipliers in their foreign and security policies, and increase the frequency of military and political consultations on climate change within NATO.

(NATO 2030, 2021, p.3)

The Arctic, for some reason, is not identified and gives the idea that it does not exist for the Alliance. Is the Cold War period a ghost presence within the organisation?

2- The Arctic region[16] within NATO

The Arctic is changing confirming that "What happens in the Arctic does not stay in the Arctic" (2017, Vidar Helgesen17). A statement that applies also in security context.
The Arctic area and region had a strategic importance during the Cold War, being highly militarized at that time. It was the shortest flight area for US and Soviet bombers. After this period and after the collapse of the USSR, a signal of cooperation approached the Arctic countries following the idea of a peace and cooperative zone expressed by Mikhail Gorbachev in 1987 in Murmansk. Gradually, NATO allies have turned their attention into other regions of the globe. The Arctic was no longer strategic and was forgotten. For the rapporteur Jean-Charles Larsonneur it was "a genuine desire to make the region one of peaceful cooperation" (2021, p. 3). According to Abbie Tingstad during the conference *Conceptualizing the Arctic; a Zone of Peace or a Zone of Conflict?* held on line on 22 november 2022, the author affirmed that "we are not looking at the same Arctic zone, there is a growing conflict"[18].

---

[16] The eight Arctic states (Canada, Denmark, Finland, Iceland, Norway, Russia, Sweden and United States) created the AEPS that became in 1996 the Arctic Council (Ottawa Declaration). The Federation of Russia is the Chair (2021-2023) of the Arctic Council. The Joint Statement of 03rd March suspended all activities with Russia due to the invasion of Ukraine. Additionally, Russia has been excluded from other forums and meetings since the illegal annexation of Crimea in 2014. (Joint Statement. (2022). https://www.state.gov/joint-statement-on-arctic-council-cooperation-following-russias-invasion-of-ukraine/).
[17] NATO. (2017). "What happens in the Arctic, does not stay in the Arctic" - climate change in the Arctic will have global consequences and cannot be ignored. https://www.nato-pa.int/news/what-happens-arctic-does-not-stay-arctic-climate-change-arctic-will-have-global-consequences
[18] Geneva Graduate Institute. (2022), November 22). co-hosted by GGC, CIES & MINT. *Conceptualizing the Arctic; a Zone of Peace or a Zone of Conflict?*. https://www.graduateinstitute.ch/communications/events/conceptualizing-arctic-zone-peace-or-zone-conflict

Though, the 21st century places this region again as an important spot. This time as a victim of the climate change, done by external anthropogenic activities that are making the temperature rising four times more in the Arctic comparing to the rest of the world, as mentioned in the introduction. The changes are visible in numerous different ways in the region: melting-ice and warmer currents from the Atlantic Ocean (known as Atlantification of the Arctic) that affects melting ice, the rise of sea level and, in its turn, allows navigability that will increase commercial transit (shorter than the Canal Suez, idem, p.4) and consequently expand economic opportunities with a ride to natural resources, more fishing and conflicts regarding territorial claims (extension of continental shelf). This interconnected scenario is placing back the Arctic region as a strategic spot, where Russia and China (the latter claiming to be an Arctic country). In this first quarter of the 21st century, both countries have been increasing their investments and research in the area. In what concerns Russia, the country has been remilitarizing, specifically since 2007, with the Arktika expedition as the first voyage to the ocean floor at the North Pole, placing its national flag. The rapporteur Jean-Charles Larsonneur highlights the Arctic Strategy 2035 of Russia, released in 2020, where there is a clear emphasis in the "necessity of guaranteeing Russia´s sovereignty and territorial integrity" and "the goal of developing the Northern Sea Route (NSR) as a globally competitive national transport corridor" (Klimenko, 2020 as cited in *idem*, p. 11). Confirming the *New Perspectives on Shared Security: NATO'S Next 70 Years* (2019) acknowledgment expressed by the author that "Moscow has built up the military capacity to complicate NATO´s ability to operate in the Black, Baltic, and North seas as well as in the North Atlantic and the Arctic" (p. 2). There has been a constant absence in the 70 years of the Alliance of this region on official documents meanwhile many growing exercises in the Arctic, namely Cold Response in Norway, the only country in the world with permanent military headquarters North of the Arctic circle (Brekke, 2022; Coffey and Kochis, 2021) reinforce the military cooperation between NATO and Arctic states. Finland and Sweden, Partners for Peace and Enhanced Partnership in Northern Europe (e-PINE, launched in 2003 by United States[19]), closely participate in NATO´s exercises. The possibility of full NATO membership is a reality since both applications in May 2022. It is clear that "the Arctic remains a vital strategic region for Euro-Atlantic security" (Charron, 2020). Due to those facts, it is almost

---

[19] In this context, "cooperation takes place in three major areas: cooperative security, healthy societies and vibrant economies" (U.S Department of state. (N.D). Enhanced Partnership in Northern Europe (E-PINE) https://www.state.gov/enhanced-partnership-in-northern-europe-e-pine/)

incomprehensible the Arctic region not expressly written in the official documents over time. Perhaps with the turning point regarding this region in the United States of America that presented its National Strategy for the Arctic Region in October 2022[20], the texts of official documents might assume, in the future, the Arctic region.

3- Conclusion

Now that, according to Causevic, NATO has "mastered in traditional security" (2017, p. 80), the Alliance needs to accelerate efforts to update climate and Arctic strategies[21] so it does not keep failing in "adopting the concept of human security" (Rico, 2022, p. 9).

To conclude, NATO should be able to look all the regions its allies, and future ones, are included in so it can properly express its real intention to protect them. If one understands that the Arctic region is also threatened by Russia and China, Finland and Sweden´s applications to NATO speak for themselves and reinforces the presence of the Arctic in the Alliance. If the organisation can make a difference with the period of the Cold War in what concerns the harsh region that is becoming more navigable, then perhaps it will be possible to look at it through a different lens and in connection with climate change. A region that has been there since its creation, with 5 of the 8 Arctic states (Canada, Iceland, Norway, USA (Alaska) and the Kingdom of Denmark (Greenland)) as part of the Alliance. In a short period of time (depending on Turkey) they will be 7 with Finland and Sweden. So, when referring to transatlantic relations (EU and North Americas) and defence, the Arctic is part of it. The oceans, Atlantic and Arctic, are meeting each other. The Arctic Council (non-traditional) and NATO (traditional) shall find a balance to work in a cooperative way in order to assure a safe and secure place for all in that region, so the "security vacuum", mentioned by NATO´s Secretary General on 25th March of 2022 at Bardufoss Air base in Norway, disappears.

Even if not expressed, the Arctic is omnipresent within NATO and climate change is acknowledged as a threat multiplier (*NATO Climate Change and Security Action Plan*

---

[20] The White House. (2022). National Strategy for the Arctic Region. https://www.whitehouse.gov/wp-content/uploads/2022/10/National-Strategy-for-the-Arctic-Region.pdf

[21] Facing this lack of strategy some scholars have been arguing and recommending different options such as: 1) Arctic Military Code of Conduct (AMCC): the authors of the Briefing Note considered it would be of relevance to define redlines (Depledge, et al. 2019); 2) According to Khorrami and Raspotnik one possibility would be direct contribution from NATO to the Permanent Structured Cooperation (PESCO) developing hybrid partnerships and agreements (2022, p. 5). Both authors highlight also the importance of the Nordic Defence Cooperation (NORDEFCO), a regional security group that include Denmark, Finland, Iceland, Norway and Sweden with the goal of strengthening participants' national defence, exploring common synergies and facilitating efficient common solutions, as mentioned in the NORDEFCO website: https://www.nordefco.org/Files/nordefco-vision-2025-signed.pdf

(number 1, 2021). The different complementary documents mentioned in this paper seem to have not been crossed and fully taken into consideration while elaborating the new Strategic Concept 2022.

References

Barry, J. (2014). Green Political Theory. In V. Geoghegan, & R. Wilford (Eds.), *Political Ideologies: An Introduction* (4 ed., pp. 153-178). Routlege. https://pureadmin.qub.ac.uk/ws/files/5420698/Green_Political_Theory_John_Barry.pdf

Brekke, K. (2022). NATO in the Arctic: Three Suggestions on NATO and Security in the Arctic. *Civita* n° 10. https://civita.no/notat/nato-in-the-arctic-three-suggestions-on-nato-and-security-in-the-arctic/

Bye, H. (2021, June 15). NATO Summit: Little reference to the Arctic, but Region still in the radar. High North News. https://www.highnorthnews.com/en/nato-summit-little-reference-arctic-region-still-radar).

Carnegie Europe. (2019). New Perspectives on Shared Security: NATO'S Next 70 Years. Tomáš Valášek, editor. https://carnegieendowment.org/files/NATO_int_final1.pdf

Causevic, A. (2017). Facing an Unpredictable Threat: Is NATO Ideally Placed to Manage Climate Change as a Non-Traditional Threat Multiplier? *The Quarterly Journal*. 16(2), pp. 59-80. DOI: https://doi.org/10.11610/Connections.16.2.04

Charron, A. (2020). NATO and the Geopolitical Future of the Arctic. *Arctic Yearbook2020*.

Coffey, L. and Kochis, D. (2021, June 10). NATO Summit 2021: The Arctic Can No Longer Be an Afterthought. Issue Brief No. 6086. *The Heritage Foundation* https://www.heritage.org/defense/report/nato-summit-2021-the-arctic-can-no-longer-be-afterthought

Cook, L. (2022, April 6). NATO Chief says Finland, Sweden welcome to apply to join. https://www.sfgate.com/news/article/NATO-chief-says-Finland-Sweden-welcome-to-apply-17061474.php)

Depledge, D. et al (2019). Why we need to talk about military activity in the Arctic: Towards an Arctic Military Code of Conduct. *Arctic Yearbook2019*.

IPCC. (2022). "Summary for Policymakers. In: Climate Change 2022: Impacts, Adaptation, and Vulnerability. Contribution of Working Group II to the Sixth Assessment Report of the Intergovernmental Panel on Climate Change. https://report.ipcc.ch/ar6/wg2/IPCC_AR6_WGII_FullReport.pdf

Khorrami, N. & Raspotnik, A. (2022, March 29). Great power competition is coming for the Arctic. NATO should prepare. *World Politics Review*. https://www.worldpoliticsreview.com/articles/30434/for-nato-russia-ukraine-war-forecasts-tensions-in-the-arctic

Koivurova, T. (2022, March 2). The war on Ukraine: consequences for Finland and the Arctic. *The Polar connection*. https://polarconnection.org/ukraine-finland-arctic/

NATO. (2010). Strategic Concept 2010 https://www.nato.int/nato_static_fl2014/assets/pdf/pdf_publications/20120214_strategic-concept-2010-eng.pdf

NATO PARLIAMENTARY ASSEMBLY. (2017, May 17). "What happens in the Arctic, does not stay in the Arctic" - climate change in the Arctic will have global consequences and cannot be ignored. https://www.nato-pa.int/news/what-happens-arctic-does-not-stay-arctic-climate-change-arctic-will-have-global-consequences

NATO PARLIAMENTARY ASSEMBLY. (2020). NATO 2030: a more united and stronger Alliance on the global stage. Declaration 460. https://www.nato-pa.int/download-file?filename=/sites/default/files/2020-12/2020%20-%20NATO%20PA%20DECLARATION%20460.pdf

NATO. (2021, June). NATO 2030. Fact Sheet. https://www.nato.int/nato_static_fl2014/assets/pdf/2021/6/pdf/2106-factsheet-nato2030-en.pdf

NATO. (2021, June 14). NATO Climate Change and Security Action Plan https://www.nato.int/cps/en/natohq/official_texts_185174.htm

NATO PARLIAMENTARY ASSEMBLY. Larsonneur J.-C. (2021). Security challenges in the High North. Report. https://www.nato-pa.int/download-file?filename=/sites/default/files/2021-10/016%20DSCTC%2021%20E%20rev.%202%20fin%20-%20SECURITY%20HIGH%20NORTH.pdf

NATO. (2022). Press conference by NATO Secretary General Jens Stoltenberg in Bardufoss, Norway for Exercise Cold Response. https://www.nato.int/cps/en/natohq/opinions_193681.htm?selectedLocale=en

Rico, L.G. (2022). NATO and Climate Change: A Climatized Perspective on Security. *Belfer Center for Science and International Affairs.* Harvard Kennedy School. https://www.belfercenter.org/publication/nato-and-climate-change-climatized-perspective-security

NATO. (2022). NATO 2022 Madrid Strategic Concept. https://www.nato.int/strategic-concept/

NATO. (2022, June 28). *Secretary General's Report, Climate Change and Security Impact Assessment.* https://www.nato.int/nato_static_fl2014/assets/pdf/2022/6/pdf/280622-climate-impact-assessment.pdf

U.S. European Command Public Affairs. (2021, November 10). Military Leaders Discuss Arctic Security, Cooperation in Annual Forum. *U.S. European Command.* https://www.eucom.mil/pressrelease/41759/military-leaders-discuss-arctic-security-cooperation-in-annual-forum

YOUR KNOWLEDGE HAS VALUE

- We will publish your bachelor's and master's thesis, essays and papers

- Your own eBook and book - sold worldwide in all relevant shops

- Earn money with each sale

Upload your text at www.GRIN.com
and publish for free